Football

PLAYERS AND TACTICS

Jim Kelman

HODDER
Wayland

an imprint of Hodder Children's Books

Other titles in the series:
Rules of the Game
Skills of the Game
Teamwork!

For more information on this series
and other Hodder Wayland titles,
go to www.hodderwayland.co.uk

Produced for Wayland
Publishers Limited by
Thunderbolt Partnership
Editor: Paula Field
Designer: Eljay Yidirim
Photography: Steve Gorton
Artwork: Phillp Morrision

First published by
Wayland Publishers Limited
This edition published in 2006
by Hodder Wayland, an imprint
of Hodder Children's Books
338 Euston Road, London
NW1 3BH

© Copyright 1999
Hodder Wayland

British Library Cataloguing
in Publication Data
Kelman, Jim
Players and Tactics. - (Soccer)
1. Soccer - Juvenile literature
1.Title 796 . 3' 34
ISBN-10: 0750249455
ISBN-13: 9780750249454

Printed in China

Foreword from Sir Clive Woodward:
For all young children who take part in the game
of football, these books will give an excellent insight
into the techniques and understanding that will help
them to become more knowledgeable and improve
their playing skills.

Contents

Introduction

Football is basically a very simple game, but there are still lots of things you will need to learn before you become a good player. You will need to know what all the markings on a football pitch mean and where you should be on the pitch.

Special skills

You will also need to know what you are expected to do in the position you play. In this book you will learn about the different types of players in a football team and discover what special skills they need to do their jobs.

▲ Football is a team game so, as well as knowing what you are doing on the pitch, you will also need to know where your team mates are so that you can pass the ball to them, or help them out if they are in trouble.

Keeping fit

Football is also a very physical game and you will have to run around a lot during each match. You will not be able to keep stopping because you are out of breath. So, if you want to play in football matches you will have to get fit. Try cycling, swimming or jogging – all these things will keep you active and build up your strength.

▲ Footballers should eat foods that provide the body with energy, such as cereals, rice, potatoes, pasta and bread.

◀ During a football match you will probably sweat a lot, so after the game, have a drink to replace this lost fluid.

The pitch and players

Most football pitches are marked with white lines so you will know where the important areas such as the touchlines are.

Divided into thirds

However, a football pitch is further divided into thirds - although there are no lines marked on the pitch. The attacking third is the area close to your opponents' goal, where your forwards try to score. The defending third is the area closest to your goal, where your defenders try to stop your opponents from scoring goals. The midfield is the area between the two.

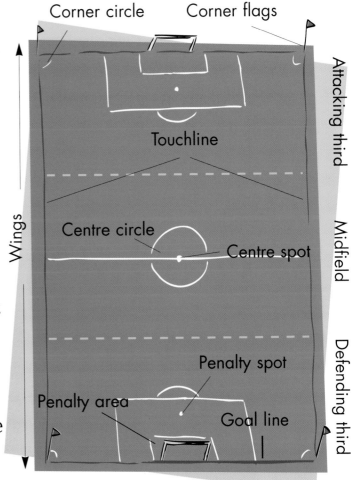

Corner circle   Corner flags

Attacking third

Touchline

Wings

Centre circle

Centre spot

Midfield

Penalty spot

Penalty area

Goal line

Defending third

The markings of a football pitch

Types of player

There are three main types of player in a team and each has a special role to play.

Defenders

Defenders play mostly in their defending third. They wear numbers 2, 3, 4 and 5. Players 2 and 3 are wide-playing full backs or wing backs. Players 4 and 5 are central defenders.

Player positions on the pitch

Midfielders

Midfield players are the link between defence and attack. They wear shirt numbers 6, 7, 8 and 11. Players 6 and 8 are central midfielders and 7 and 11 are often wide players.

Attackers

Attackers push into the attacking third trying to score goals. Attackers wear shirt numbers 9 and 10.

Warming up and down

The more active you are, the harder your body works – your muscles use up a lot of energy, your heart beats faster and your temperature rises. It is vital to prepare your body for these changes, so you must warm up.

▼ Star jumps

Star jumps are a good way to warm up.

▶ Waist

Put your arm up above your head and bend gently from side to side.

Warming up

Before doing hard exercise, warm up your muscles using stretches. Don't strain – do the stretches gently. Do these stretches before and after a game and hold them for 6-10 seconds.

◀ Lower calf

Place one foot in front of the other, facing forward. Bend both knees, keeping heels on the ground. Feel the stretch in your lower calf.

▶ Back of thigh

Bend your left leg with hands on the knee. Put your right leg forward and bend forwards, with your weight on the bent leg. Feel the stretch behind your right thigh. Repeat with the other leg.

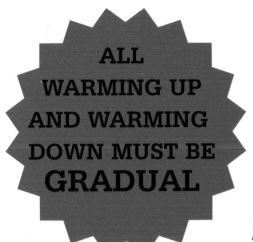

▶Lower back

Lie on your back with your arms spread out. Bend your legs and move them together from one side of your body to the other. Feel the stretch in your lower back.

◀ Bottom

Sit on the floor and put your right leg over your left leg. Now pull it across your chest and repeat with the other leg. Feel the stretch in your bottom.

Warming down

After your training or football game, it is now time to relax. Warming down (cooling down) is good for your body, so make it a habit after every period of vigorous exercise.

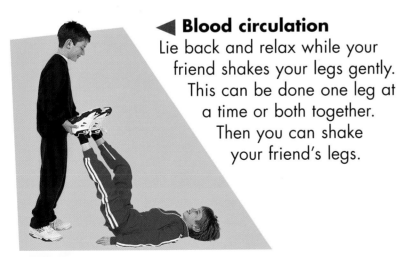

◀ Blood circulation

Lie back and relax while your friend shakes your legs gently. This can be done one leg at a time or both together. Then you can shake your friend's legs.

▲ Keeping warm

You do not want your body to get chilled so always put on some extra clothes after a match.

The goalkeeper

To play in goal you must have courage, agility, balance and the ability to out-think your opponents.

Head up

Upper body straight

Elbows tucked in

Hands slightly open at waist height

Knees bent

Feet shoulder-width apart

Weight on balls of feet

Ready and alert

A goalkeeper should always be alert and ready to move in any direction. By standing in the correct position, you will be balanced and able to move quickly.

Check your position

When you are in goal, keep checking your position and also where the ball is. Apart from penalty kicks, you should never stand on your own goal line.

◀ Always stay in the alert position until you make the decision to move.

The goalkeeper's position

10

Where to stand

If the ball is at the other end of the pitch, stay on the edge of your own penalty area. As play gets closer, move back to your goal – you might have to deal with a shot, so keep alert.

▶ Sometimes one of your defenders will stand on your goal line. If you don't make the save, your team mate may be able to get the ball away.

▲ Narrowing the angle

Time your move carefully. If you come out too soon, your opponent can dribble the ball round you. If you come out too far, he may chip the ball over your head.

Narrow the angle

As an attacker approaches with the ball, come off your line – this will make the goal area seem smaller. If you stay on your line you give the attacker a larger target to shoot at and a good chance of scoring.

STOPPING THE BALL

As the goalkeeper your job is to keep the ball out of the net. It doesn't matter how you do this, you can use your hands to catch the ball or punch it away, or you can stop the ball using your legs and feet.

▶ Diving
If the ball is a long way from you, you might have to dive to catch or knock it away.

▶ Cushioning
Once you have caught the ball bring it into your body to keep it safe.

▲ Catching
When you catch the ball above chest height, make sure your fingers are spread out and your thumbs are at the back and sides of the ball.

◀ Punching

If the ball is too high to catch, punch it back in the direction it came. To punch the ball, clench both fists tightly together and keep your wrists firm.

▶ Smothering

Sometimes you will need to dive right at an attacker's feet to save the ball. When you smother a ball, make sure you get your timing right – too soon and the attacker might kick the ball over you, too late and the ball may slip underneath you.

◀ Deflecting

If the ball is too close to the goal and you cannot catch or punch it away, use the palm of your hand or your fingers to tip it over the bar. When deflecting the ball be careful that the ball does not rebound off the post and back into play.

A GREAT GOALKEEPER IS ALWAYS READY FOR THE BALL

The defender

As a defender your main duties are to stop the opposition from attacking, blocking shots and clearing the ball out of danger.

Staying 'goal side'

When defending you must always stay 'goal side'. This means placing yourself between the attacker and your goal. This is a good defending position.

▲ As a defender you will have to 'jockey' your opponent. This means getting in his way and slowing him down.

◀ **Staying goal side**
Defender (1) runs to get between attacker (2) and his own goal, putting him in a good position to make a challenge.

Defenders often need to mark their opponents closely. They need to follow them up and down the pitch and have to change speed and direction quickly.

Challenging for the ball

As a defender you will need to challenge your opponent for the ball. The most direct way to win the ball is to tackle your opponent, but it is better to intercept the ball as you will have more control.

▼ If your opponents have been awarded a direct free kick in front of your goal, you will need a defensive wall to block the shot. The wall should cover as much of the goal as possible without blocking the keeper's view.

▲ If you don't think you can intercept the ball stay in your goal-side position. Only make a tackle as a last resort.

Defence into attack

A good defender can also turn defence into attack. Try to get the ball out of your defending third and into your opponents' half.

The defender's role

When your opponents have the ball, everyone in your team must defend. However, the defensive players have a special role to play.

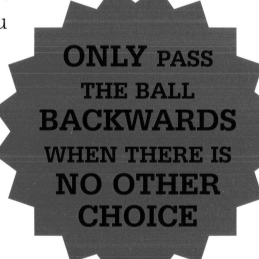

In football the only body contact allowed is the shoulder charge. The defender (blue and white) is using only the top part of her arm to nudge her opponent out of the way. Her elbows are out of the way and the ball is within playing distance.

When your team has the ball, you and your team mates should move into positions that make it easier to pass the ball and move it to the attackers. Once the forwards have the ball, move forward to support your team mates. Sometimes a defender can go all the way forward to try and score!

ONLY PASS THE BALL BACKWARDS WHEN THERE IS NO OTHER CHOICE

Back passes

Defenders will sometimes pass the ball back to their goalkeeper. Most will only do this if they want to pass the ball upfield but are surrounded by opposition players.

▲ The goalkeeper can't pick up a kicked-back pass, he has to kick the ball away instead.

Under pressure

Never pass the ball across the goalmouth, as your opponents might be able to run in quickly and score a goal. If your goalkeeper is under pressure (if there are opposition strikers nearby) kick the ball out of play. If you pass to the goalie when an attacker might get to it, the opposition might sneak a goal. It's far better to give away a throw-in or corner.

▲ Forcing play

Player 1 forces his opponent (2) to take the ball down the line. Player (2) now only has one option – to cross the ball. If he had come inside the defender, he would have been able to pass or shoot.

17

The midfielder

As a midfield player, you are in the middle of a game that it going on all around you. You are the link between defence and attack and will have to run all over the field to help out your attackers, defenders and wide players.

Good vision

You must have good vision. This means that before you get the ball, you should know what you are going to do with it.

Passing and scoring

Midfielders often pass the ball to a team mate who is better at scoring goals, or is in a better position, but you might get the opportunity to score a goal yourself.

▲ This England midfielder leaps into the air to get a foot to the ball before his Chilean opponent can reach it.

Tracking a player

When you are defending, the opposing midfield player will be trying to get forward. So you must mark him. If he runs forward, then you must go with him. This is called 'tracking a player' and is a vital part of your game.

▲ The midfielder's path to goal has been blocked by a defender. He has to decide whether to take the ball on himself and try to score or pass the ball to a team mate who is in a better position to score.

A MIDFIELDER NEEDS GOOD VISION

▲ Track your opponent as closely as you can and always be ready to challenge for the ball to win back possession.

THE PASSING GAME

When your team has the ball it is vital that you keep possession. Get into a position where your team mate can pass the ball to you – make sure he or she can pass the ball forwards, rather than across the pitch.

THINK BEFORE YOU PASS!

A wall pass

If you are closely marked, try a wall pass, also called a one-two. You will have to pass the ball to a team mate, then run around your opponent and find a space where you can pick up the return pass from the same player.

▼ **A wall pass**
Player 1 has passed the ball to his team mate (2) and quickly run around the defender (3) into a space where player (2) has returned the pass to him.

Helping out

When possession changes from team to team, keep an eye on the player you are marking, but also be aware of what your defence is doing. If they are struggling, you might need to be prepared to drop back to help them out. You can pick up the player you were marking again as he or she comes forward.

▲ **Being compact**
Because the blues have reduced the amount of empty space in the middle of the pitch, the attackers (yellow) will have to pass the ball around, or over, the defence, which may give the blue team the opportunity to win back the ball.

The wide player

If you play in a wide position (along the edges of the pitch) you have to cover a lot of ground and be first to the ball, which means you have to be a fast runner.

Running with the ball

Once you have the ball, you must be good at running with the ball and crossing or shooting.

▲ England's Michael Owen uses his pace and his ball skills to beat a tackle from Chile's Ronald Fuentes on the edge of the pitch.

Attack or defence

To be a wide player, you may be in the position of full back or winger. You can, however, be a combination of the two – a wing back. The touchline will always be fairly close to you, so you will need good control and to be good at dribbling so that you can keep the ball in play.

▲ Winger

As a winger (1) you will run up and down the edge of the pitch with the ball, trying to cross it to your team mates or score yourself. The opposition full back (2) will be trying to stop you.

▲ Wing back

As a wing back (1) you will have to challenge attacks on the wing. You need to be strong to clear the ball out of danger and able to 'jockey' opposition attackers on the wing.

CROSSING THE BALL

When you are in the attacking third of the pitch, you will be expected to go past opposition players and either shoot or cross the ball.

A cross

A cross is a ball played from either wing to the middle of the pitch or into the goalmouth for a striker to run on to.

▲ Get into a good wide position with the ball and run as fast as you can, pushing the ball ahead so that you do not have to check your stride.

Finding space

When your team has possession, you must try to get forward and support your attacking players by finding space on the wing where they can get the ball to you.

A HIGH PERCENTAGE OF GOALS ARE SCORED FROM **CROSSES**

Making decisions

As a wide player you must be able to make decisions. You must quickly make up your mind about when and where to cross the ball (will it go to the near post or far post?) and which type of cross to make (low or high, an 'inswinger' or an 'outswinger'?).

▶ Inswinging cross/corner

An inswinging cross or corner curls in towards the goal. A right-footed player will take an inswinger from the left of the goal, while a left-footed player will take it from the right side of the goal.

◀ Outswinging cross/corner

An outswinging cross or corner curls away from the goal. This type of cross makes it easier for a team mate to run on to the ball. A left-footed player will take an outswinger from the left of the goal, while a right-footed player will take it from the right side of the goal.

The striker

The striker is the player who gets most of the glory! What does it take to become a great striker? You must be quick and able to twist and turn to make yourself hard to mark. If you can lose your marker you will be in a good position to receive the ball and try to score.

▲ ▶

If you want to get the ball in the back of the net, try not to look in the direction you plan to shoot. Your opponents may see where you are aiming the ball.

The first touch

As a striker, you must be able to control the ball with your first touch so that when you receive the ball, you can shoot straight away or pass it to a team mate.

Keeping control

You must be able to keep control of the ball, even when you are being challenged by an opponent.

Playing into space

Sometimes the ball is played into the space behind the defenders. If this happens, the striker will need to be quick to get to the ball before the opposition.

▲ Back to goal

Strikers play a lot of the time with their back to the opposition's goal so that they can see the ball coming. If you receive the ball with your back to the goal (1), you will need to be able to turn quickly to shoot.

SHOOTING SKILLS

As the striker your opponents will be marking you tightly. When your team has possession, they will want to pass the ball to you, so you will need to lose your marker and then outwit the goalkeeper.

When to score

Goals can be scored from planned set pieces, where the rest of the team are involved in getting the ball to you in a certain way, or just by spotting an opportunity.

▲ To do a half-volley, kick the ball just as it bounces. If you strike the ball correctly, the shot will be powerful and the ball should stay low.

IF YOU DON'T SHOOT YOU WILL NEVER SCORE!

Ways to score

You will need to master the ways of shooting the ball, such as chipping or heading, as you will need to use these techniques. If the ball coming towards you is high, you can use the volley or half-volley to shoot.

Shoot on sight

You may try to score using a sliding shot, an overhead kick or, if you are feeling brave, by heading the ball into the net. But the most important things are knowing where the goal is without having to look for it and being prepared to shoot at every opportunity.

▲ Some strikers do overhead kicks when they have their back to goal. It is a very exciting kick, but can also be dangerous. Never attempt an overhead kick unless you have been properly trained.

▲ If a defender is trying to clear the ball from the goal area, try a sliding shot. Slide to one side of the defender and stretch your leg as far forward as you can, scooping the ball into the net with your other foot.

Confidence

Confidence is probably the most important skill for you to develop. Every time there is an opportunity to shoot or head the ball towards goal, you must take it! Your self-belief – and your ball skills – will help you to become an outstanding player.

 Glossary

Attackers Forward players who play in the attacking third of the pitch.

Attacking third The area of the pitch where the attackers try to score goals.

Back pass When a player passes the ball back to his goalkeeper.

Centre A circle in the middle of the pitch, from where the kick-off is taken.

Cross A ball played from either wing to the middle of the pitch.

Cushioning A goalkeeping technique – when the keeper brings the ball into his body to keep it safe.

Defenders Players who prevent the opposition from scoring goals.

Defending third The area of the pitch where defenders try to stop their opponents from scoring.

Deflecting A goalkeeping technique – when the keeper tips the ball over the bar.

Diving A goalkeeping technique – when the keeper has to save a low ball.

Forcing play Forcing your opponent to take the ball wide to give him or her less attacking options.

Full back Defenders who usually wear shirt numbers 2 and 3.

Goalkeeper The player who tries to keep the ball out of the net.

Goal line The white line that marks the edge of the short side of the pitch.

Goal side A good defending position. The defender places himself between his own goal and his opponent.

Inswinger A type of cross, often taken from a corner.

Jockeying Getting in your opponent's way and slowing him down.

Midfield The middle third of the pitch, between defence and attack.

Midfielders Players who are the link between the attack and the defence.

Narrowing the angle A goalkeeper's tactic to make it difficult for an attacker to score.

Outswinger A type of cross, often coming from a corner.

Penalty area The white box around the goal. The edge of the penalty area is 16.5m from the goal line.

Penalty spot A mark on the pitch, from where penalty kicks are taken. It is 11m from the goal line.

Punching A goalkeeping technique – when the keeper uses his fists to punch the ball away.

Smothering A goalkeeping technique – when the keeper dives at an attacker's feet

Striker The player whose main job is to score goals.

Sweeper A player who runs the width of the pitch behind his defenders, sweeping up any loose balls.

Touchline The white lines that mark out the edge of the long side of the pitch.

Tracking a player Marking an opponent by following them up and down the pitch.

Wall pass A passing move, where you pass the ball to a team mate and then run into a position to pick up the return pass. Also called a one-two.

Warming up and down Important exercises to do before and after any vigorous exercise.

Wide player A player who plays on the wings. Also called a winger.

Wing back A combination of a winger and a full back.

Further Information

Football Associations

English F.A., 25 Soho Square, London W1D 4FA
www.thefa.com

Scottish F.A., Hampden Park, Glasgow G42 9AY
www.scottishfa.co.uk

F.A. of Wales, Plymouth Chambers, 3 Westgate Street, Cardiff CF10 1DP
www.fawtrust.org.uk

Irish F.A. (Northern Ireland), 20 Windsor Avenue, Belfast BT9 6EG
www.irishfa.com

F.A. of Ireland (Republic of Ireland), 80 Merreon Square, Dubin 2
www.fai.ie

Books

Defensive Soccer Tactics by Jens Bangbo and Berger Pietersen
(Human Kinetics Europe, 2001)
SAQ Soccer: Speed, Agility and Quickness for Soccer
by Alan Pearson (A&C Black, 2001)
The Football Association Coaching Book of Soccer Tactics and Skills by
Charles Hughes (Queen Anne Press, 1994)
The Practices and Training Sessions of the World's Top Teams and Coaches
by Mike Saif (Reedswain Incorporated, 2000)
Youth Soccer Drills by Jim Garland (Human Kinetics Europe, 2003)

Index